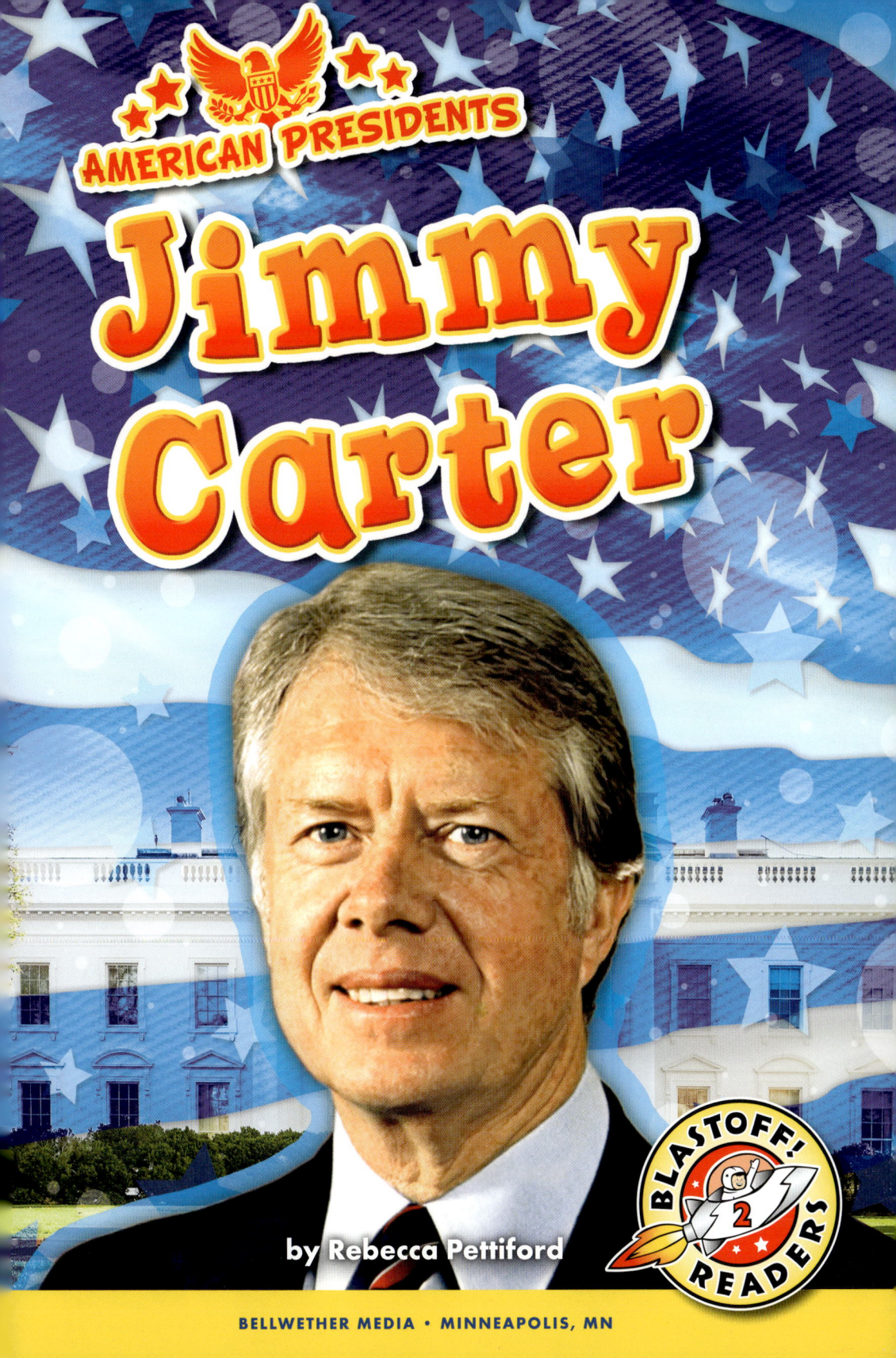

Blastoff! Readers are carefully developed by literacy experts to build reading stamina and move students toward fluency by combining standards-based content with developmentally appropriate text.

 **Level 1** provides the most support through repetition of high-frequency words, light text, predictable sentence patterns, and strong visual support.

 **Level 2** offers early readers a bit more challenge through varied sentences, increased text load, and text-supportive special features.

 **Level 3** advances early-fluent readers toward fluency through increased text load, less reliance on photos, advancing concepts, longer sentences, and more complex special features.

★ **Blastoff! Universe**

Reading Level

 Grade K

 Grades 1–3

 Grade 4

This edition first published in 2023 by Bellwether Media, Inc.

No part of this publication may be reproduced in whole or in part without written permission of the publisher. For information regarding permission, write to Bellwether Media, Inc., Attention: Permissions Department, 6012 Blue Circle Drive, Minnetonka, MN 55343.

Library of Congress Cataloging-in-Publication Data

Names: Pettiford, Rebecca, author.
Title: Jimmy Carter / by Rebecca Pettiford.
Description: Minneapolis, MN : Bellwether Media, Inc., 2023. | Series: Blastoff! readers: American presidents | Includes bibliographical references and index. | Audience: Ages 5-8 | Audience: Grades 2-3 | Summary: "Relevant images match informative text in this introduction to Jimmy Carter. Intended for students in kindergarten through third grade"-- Provided by publisher.
Identifiers: LCCN 2022001068 (print) | LCCN 2022001069 (ebook) | ISBN 9781644877074 (library binding) | ISBN 9781648348730 (paperback) | ISBN 9781648347535 (ebook)
Subjects: LCSH: Carter, Jimmy, 1924---Juvenile literature. | Presidents--United States--Biography--Juvenile literature.
Classification: LCC E873 .P48 2023 (print) | LCC E873 (ebook) | DDC 973.926092 [B]--dc23/eng/20220112
LC record available at https://lccn.loc.gov/2022001068
LC ebook record available at https://lccn.loc.gov/2022001069

Text copyright © 2023 by Bellwether Media, Inc. BLASTOFF! READERS and associated logos are trademarks and/or registered trademarks of Bellwether Media, Inc.

Editor: Rachael Barnes   Series Designer: Jeffrey Kollock   Designer: Gabriel Hilger

Printed in the United States of America, North Mankato, MN.

Table of Contents

Who Is Jimmy Carter?	4
Time in Office	12
What Jimmy Left Behind	20
Glossary	22
To Learn More	23
Index	24

Who Is Jimmy Carter?

Jimmy Carter was the 39th president of the United States. He served from 1977 to 1981.

He was the first president born in a hospital!

Jimmy and his wife, Rosalynn

Jimmy was born in Georgia in 1924. His family had a peanut farm.

Jimmy liked to learn. He studied at two Georgia **universities**.

Jimmy went to a military school. Then he joined the U.S. **Navy**.

Presidential Picks

Foods

steak, cornbread, and fried chicken

Hobby

woodworking

Sports

basketball and tennis

Music

country and bluegrass

His father died in 1953. Jimmy left the navy to run the family farm.

From 1963 to 1967, Jimmy was a Georgia **senator**. He became **governor** in 1971.

Jimmy stood for **equality**. He created government jobs for Black people and women.

Time in Office

In the 1970s, people were out of work. Prices were high.

Jimmy ran for president. He was **elected** in 1976. People believed he could help!

Question

What helped Jimmy become president?

The **energy** supply was low in the 1970s. Jimmy asked people to **conserve** it.

Presidential Profile

Place of Birth

Plains, Georgia

Schooling
Georgia Institute of Technology and U.S. Naval Academy

Birthday
October 1, 1924

Term
1977 to 1981

Party

Democratic

Signature

Vice President

Walter Mondale

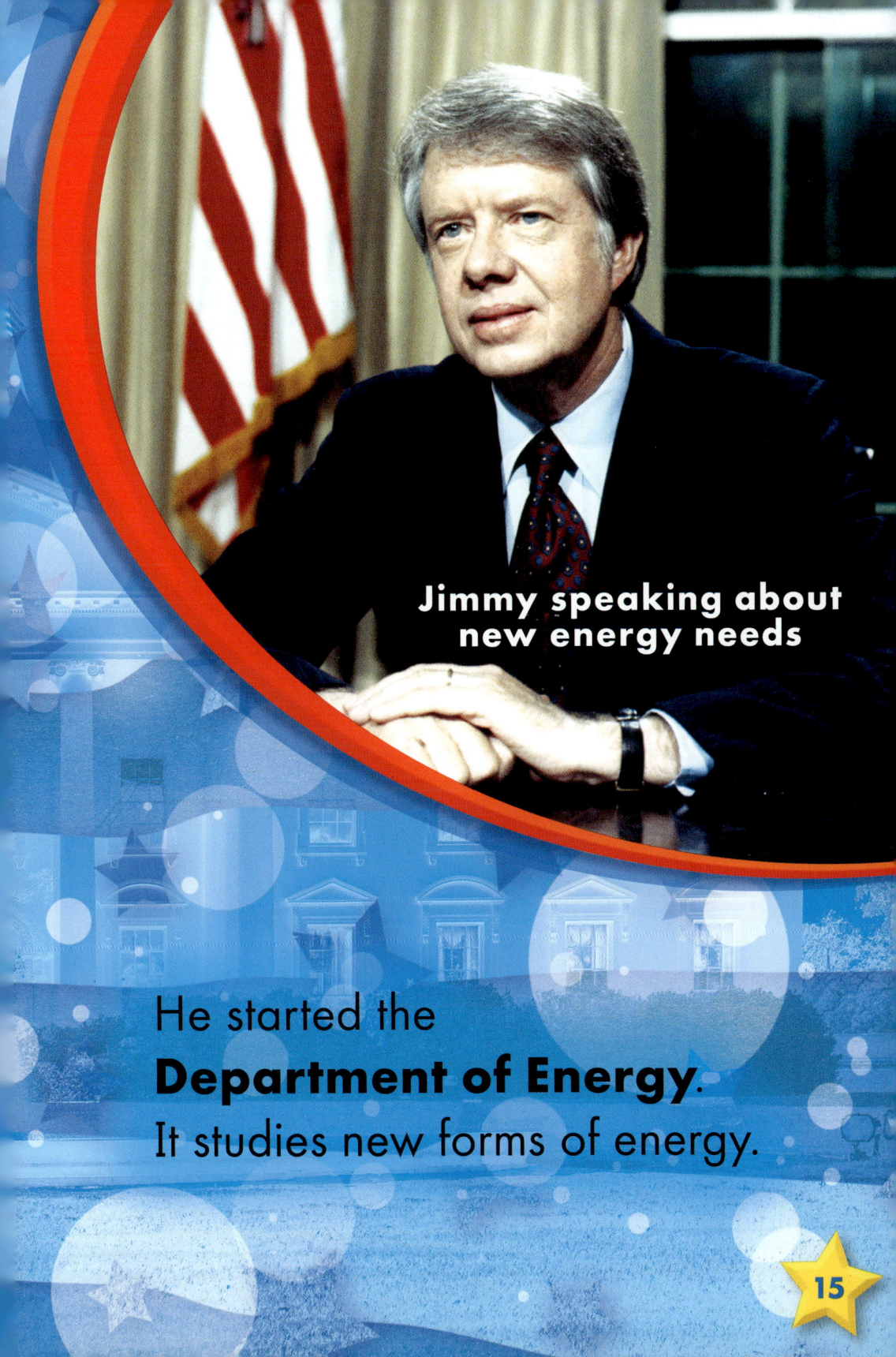

Jimmy speaking about new energy needs

He started the **Department of Energy**. It studies new forms of energy.

In 1978, Egypt and Israel did not get along. Jimmy wanted to help.

He started the **Camp David Accords**. The two countries agreed to peace.

In 1979, Americans were taken **hostage** in Iran. Jimmy worked to free them peacefully.

His plan failed. People lost hope in Jimmy.

Jimmy Timeline

November 2, 1976

Jimmy Carter is elected president

August 4, 1977

The Department of Energy is formed

September 17, 1978

Jimmy and leaders from Egypt and Israel sign the Camp David Accords

April 1980

The plan to save American hostages in Iran fails

November 4, 1980

Jimmy loses reelection to Ronald Reagan

January 20, 1981

Jimmy leaves office

What Jimmy Left Behind

Jimmy left office in 1981. While president, he worked for human **rights** and peace.

He continues to help people around the world!

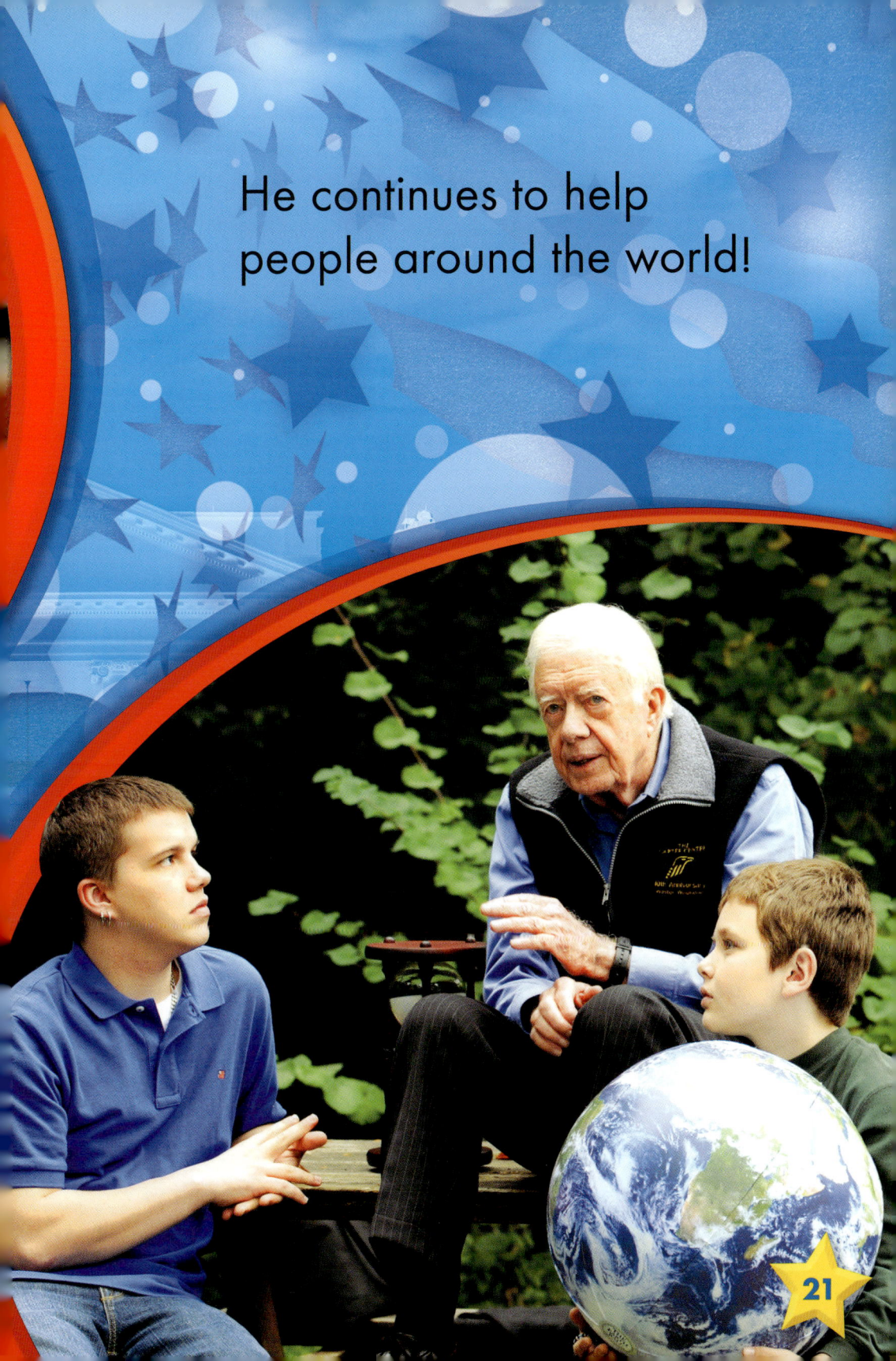

Glossary

Camp David Accords—an agreement that helped build peace between Egypt and Israel

conserve—to save something or stop the waste of it

Department of Energy—a part of the U.S. government formed in 1977 to study and make rules about energy

elected—chosen by voting

energy—usable power that comes from heat, electricity, oil, and other sources

equality—the state of everyone having the same rights and respect

governor—the leader of the government of a state

hostage—taken against a person's will; hostages are people who are often set free when traded for money or actions.

navy—the part of a country's military that fights at sea

rights—things that every person should be allowed to have, get, or do

senator—a member of the senate; the senate helps make laws.

universities—schools that people go to after high school

To Learn More

AT THE LIBRARY

Hegedus, Bethany. *Hard Work, But It's Worth It: The Life of Jimmy Carter.* New York, N.Y.: Balzar + Bray, 2020.

Messner, Kate. *The Next President: The Unexpected Beginnings and Unwritten Future of American Presidents.* San Francisco, Calif.: Chronicle Books, 2020.

Rustad, Martha E.H. *The President of the United States.* North Mankato, Minn.: Pebble, 2020.

ON THE WEB

FACTSURFER

Factsurfer.com gives you a safe, fun way to find more information.

1. Go to www.factsurfer.com.

2. Enter "Jimmy Carter" into the search box and click 🔍.

3. Select your book cover to see a list of related content.

Index

Camp David Accords, 17
conserve, 14
Department of Energy, 15
Egypt, 16
elected, 12
energy, 14, 15
equality, 11
family, 5, 6, 9
Georgia, 6, 7, 10
governor, 10
hometown, 7
hospital, 5
hostage, 18
human rights, 20
Iran, 18

Israel, 16
jobs, 11
peace, 17, 18, 20
peanut farm, 6, 9
picks, 8
profile, 14
question, 13
senator, 10
timeline, 19
universities, 7
U.S. Navy, 8, 9

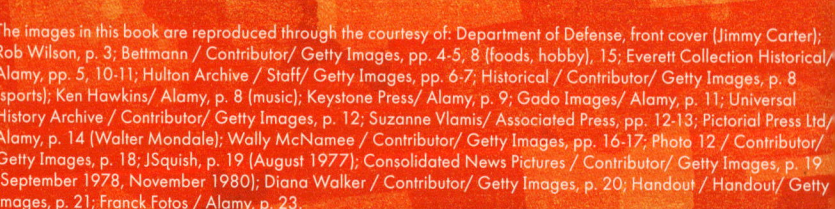

The images in this book are reproduced through the courtesy of: Department of Defense, front cover (Jimmy Carter); Rob Wilson, p. 3; Bettmann / Contributor/ Getty Images, pp. 4-5; 8 (foods, hobby), 15; Everett Collection Historical, Alamy, pp. 5, 10-11; Hulton Archive / Staff/ Getty Images, pp. 6-7; Historical / Contributor/ Getty Images, p. 8 (sports); Ken Hawkins/ Alamy, p. 8 (music); Keystone Press/ Alamy, p. 9; Gado Images/ Alamy, p. 11; Universal History Archive / Contributor/ Getty Images, p. 12; Suzanne Vlamis/ Associated Press, pp. 12-13; Pictorial Press Ltd/ Alamy, p. 14 (Walter Mondale); Wally McNamee / Contributor/ Getty Images, pp. 16-17; Photo 12 / Contributor/ Getty Images, p. 18; JSquish, p. 19 (August 1977); Consolidated News Pictures / Contributor/ Getty Images, p. 19 (September 1978, November 1980); Diana Walker / Contributor/ Getty Images, p. 20; Handout / Handout/ Getty Images, p. 21; Franck Fotos / Alamy, p. 23.